Gargling W Jelly—The Play!

Brian Patten

Samuel French - London
New York - Toronto - Hollywood

GARGLING WITH JELLY — THE PLAY!

First produced by Hull Truck Theatre Company at
Spring Street Theatre, Hull, on December 6th, 1988, with
the following cast of characters:

Jimmy	Nick Lane
Dad	Andrew Livingstone
Mum	Catherine Dow-Blyton
Mrs Scattybags	Catherine Dow-Blyton
Dr Sensible	Andrea Thomson

Directed by John Godber
Designed by Liz Ashcroft

SYNOPSIS OF SCENES

PRODUCTION NOTE

There are as many ways of staging a play as there are plays. While Hull Truck's production had Jimmy's kitchen as the main set, onto which a hospital trolley etc. could be wheeled to denote Dr Sensible's clinic, a subsequent Liverpool Everyman Theatre production had the clinic as the main set onto which a TV etc. could be wheeled to denote Jimmy's kitchen. The clinic's operating table became Jimmy's bed etc.

While Hull Truck's production was bright and cartoon-like, with a separate "city" backdrop that unfolded in front of the kitchen, the Everyman production made more use of lights—the doctor's clinic and the outside world becoming awash with purples and blues, giving the sense of a cold, metallic clinic and a futuristic world.

The play can be performed whenever, but for Christmas productions Dr Sensible's ban on birthdays can be down-played and her ban on Christmas presents highlighted. Obviously, if it is a Christmas production, Father Christmas won't be decked out in his holiday gear. The lyrics can be treated as either spoken poems or set to music as songs.

Brian Patten

CHARACTERS

Jimmy, a young boy
Mum
Dad
Dr Sensible, a wicked Doctor
Mrs Scattybags, Dr Sensible's sister
1st Reporter
2nd Reporter
Dr Sensible's Assistant
The Headless Body
Prime Minister
Policeman

Extras: **Headless bodies, Men in white coats**

This play can be performed by a cast of five

ACT I

Dr Sensible's Clinic

Darkness. Voices shouting "Jimmy!" "Where are you, lad?" Sudden tight spotlight up on Dad shouting for Jimmy. Snap Black-out. Elsewhere, a sudden tight spotlight comes up on Dr Sensible, laughing. Snap Black-out. Elsewhere, a sudden tight spotlight comes up on Mum calling for Jimmy. Snap Black-out

Jimmy bursts on to the stage out of breath. He is wearing a long grey coat and a grey cap

Jimmy Shush. Quiet. I don't want Dr Sensible to find me. My name's Jimmy and I've just been poisoned. Well, not poisoned exactly but tricked into taking some terrible medicine. It makes children turn grey and heartless. They don't want to play or have any fun. I was tricked into taking it by Dr Sensible. She hates children. This is her clinic. Just one drop of her evil medicine and gazoom—you're done for. You become mean and selfish, just like her. She's already given it to thousands and thousands of children, and now it's working on me. Soon I won't be able to see or hear you anymore. I'll be just like the groanups (*sic*). I must find the antidote. If I don't, every single child on the planet will be forced to take her medicine.

The sound of Dr Sensible's manic laughter. A door opens and slams closed

It's her. She's around somewhere. I must find the cure. Listen, I think the best thing to do, before I grow too serious to want to talk to you, is explain the whole story, right from the beginning. It all began a few days before my birthday.

Scene change music

SCENE 2

Jimmy's living-room/kitchen. There are grey pictures on the walls, greyish furniture etc. Mum and Dad are slumped in front of the TV. They look a little grey. Jimmy takes off his sensible coat and puts on a bright, fashionable bomber jacket. He sits at a table scribbling

Jimmy I was sitting writing a poem instead of doing my homework.
Dad (*without turning*) What are you doing?
Jimmy My homework.

Mum That's nice.

Dad As long as you're not writing one of those daft poems or day-dreaming. You're too much of a day-dreamer, you are.

Mum You used to be a day-dreamer yourself, Dad. There were lots of things you dreamed of doing.

Dad Like climbing mountains . . .

Mum And swimming the Channel single-handed . . .

Dad And playing football for Liverpool.

Jimmy And writing poetry?

Dad And writing poe . . . Enough of your cheek. It's been proven writing poetry and day-dreaming is bad for you. Dr Sensible said so on television last night. That's one of the reasons why she invented her famous medicine.

Mum and Dad go back to staring at the TV, assuming frozen positions

Jimmy (*secretly to the audience*) I've nearly finished a poem. What rhymes with hitch? Ditch? Pitch? Any other words? (*He leads them to the word "witch"*) Witch! That's a good rhyme. The poem's about an imaginary little sister.

Jimmy performs "Trouble With My Sister", allowing the audience to say the last word

> My little sister was truly awful,
> She was really shocking,
> She put the budgie in the fridge
> And slugs in Mummy's stocking.
>
> She was really awful,
> But it was a load of fun
> When she stole Uncle Wilbur's
> Double-barrelled gun.
>
> She aimed it at a pork pie
> And blew it into bits,
> She aimed at a hamster
> That was having fits.
>
> She leapt upon the telly,
> She pirouetted on the cat,
> She gargled with some jelly
> And spat in Grandad's hat.
>
> She ran down the hallway,
> She ran across the road,
> She dug up lots of little worms
> And caught a squirming toad.
>
> She put them in a large pot
> And she began to stir,
> She added a pint of bat's blood
> And some rabbit fur.

> She leapt upon the Hoover,
> Around the room she went,
> Once she had a turned-up nose
> But now her nose is bent.
>
> I like my little sister,
> There is really just one hitch,
> I think my little sister
> Has become a little WITCH!

Dad I thought you were doing your homework?

Jimmy I was.

Dad You weren't. You were reading one of your daft poems to yourself.

Jimmy I wasn't. I was reading it to the kids.

Dad Kids? What kids? There are no kids here. Mum, can you see any children anywhere?

Mum There's Jimmy.

Dad I mean besides Jimmy.

Mum (*unsure*) No ... not unless you say so, Dad. (*Firmer*) No, there are absolutely no children here except our Jimmy.

The audience are likely to disagree

Jimmy It's no use shouting at them. I'm the only one who can see and hear you—the groanups can't. They took some of Dr Sensible's medicine when they were little. I wouldn't waste my breath on them. But if any of the groanups do anything you think I should know about, you'll tell me, won't you? Otherwise, don't argue with them, it's useless.

Dad sees Jimmy talking

Dad That's the last straw, Jimmy. I've had enough of you talking to your imaginary friends. From now on all your day-dreaming has got to stop. Otherwise I'm going to call in Dr Sensible.

Dr Sensible music

Jimmy Not Dr Sensible, Dad. Not her!

Dad I will. And you know what her anti-day-dreaming medicine tastes like, don't you? Like pulverized frogs.

Mum More like boiled mice, dear. She gave me some when I was little.

Dad Pulverized frogs. I had it as well. It did me the world of good—I think.

Jimmy Aw, don't, Dad. All the kids I know are scared stiff of her. (*To the audience*) Mind you, all my friends have been acting a bit strange lately, as if they sort of don't mind her anymore. It's weird!

Dad Then promise me you'll stop day-dreaming.

Jimmy nods and yawns

Dad OK. Come on, time for bed.

Jimmy Have you remembered my birthday present for tomorrow?

Dad Of course, son. Now, bed.

Mum and Dad exit

Fade Lights to bedroom area. Jimmy gets ready for bed

Jimmy (*to the audience*) Well, I promised Dad I'd try my best to stop day-dreaming, but when you're as big a day-dreamer as me, it's not the easiest promise to keep. (*Shouting off*) Good-night Mum, good-night Dad.

Jimmy climbs into bed, turns on a bedside lamp and picks up a book

Now, where was I up to? "The Return of the Headless Ghost". The ghost's head was looking for a new body to fix itself on to ...

Jimmy reads then dozes off. Dream music. The Lights change

Somewhere above him, on top of a cupboard perhaps, a severed head appears. Elsewhere, a headless ghost materializes. The head begins singing and a procession of different headless bodies might cross the stage, or appear and disappear, under his bed, each body being rejected by the head

Head	I tried a sailor's body But was sea-sick all the time, I tried a policeman's body But then indulged in crime.
	I tried a cowboy's body But couldn't shoot a gun, I tried a teacher's body But it wasn't any fun.
Bodies	It wants its own body back, Even in a sack, Even if the bones are broken It wants its own body back.
Head	I tried a murderer's body But felt guilty every day, I tried a poet's body But found I could not make anything rhyme at all.
	I tried a judge's body But the wig did not fit. I tried a boxer's body But all I got was hit.
Bodies	It wants its own body back, Even in a sack, Even if the bones are broken It wants its own body back.
Head	I tried a pop star's body But found I could not sing. I tried a wrestler's body But got thrown out of the ring.

                        I tried a dustman's body
                        But could not stand the smell.
                        I tried an angel's body
                        But ended up in hell.

Bodies   It wants its own body back,
                        Even in a sack,
                        Even if the bones are broken
                        It wants its own body back.

Fade to Black-out

                              SCENE 3

The next morning. Jimmy wakes. Still dozy, he gets out of bed and opens the bathroom cabinet. A hand reaches out and offers him a toothbrush which he takes, matter of factly. He brushes his teeth and the hand takes the toothbrush back. Jimmy closes the cabinet

Dad (*off*) Up you get, sleepy head. Don't hang about day-dreaming.

Jimmy Great! It's my birthday. Hope dad's got the right bike.(*He crosses to the kitchen area*)

Mum and Dad enter looking crestfallen. Dad is carrying a pair of handlebars from a bicycle

What's up?

Mum gives Dad a you-tell-him look

Dad I've just been dismantling your birthday present. It was the most fantastic racing bike ever. But birthdays and birthday presents have been cancelled.

Jimmy Cancelled?

Mum You can still grow old and wrinkly but you don't get any presents for doing it.

Jimmy You can't ban birthdays. Not birthdays.

Dad Dr Sensible was on TV again last night. She's convinced the Government that having fun and birthdays are not very sensible. She's also got them to ban Christmas.

Mum She says having fun is a childish waste of time. The Government have all taken her medicine so they agree with her. It's official. Birthdays are kaput. Out the window. Demolished. Banned.

Jimmy Do you agree with her, Dad?

Dad Er ... Mmmmm ... Do we, Mum?

Mum I don't know, Dad. I suppose we should, if the Government says so.

Jimmy I hate Dr Sensible.

Mum ⎱
Dad ⎰ (*together, fearfully*) Shush.

Dad (*awkwardly*) There's something else as well, Jimmy.

He looks at Mum. She nods

You had another nightmare last night, didn't you?

Jimmy shakes his head

Dad You did.
Jimmy No, it was a fantastic dream.
Dad You're wasting your life in never-never land, Jimmy.
Mum After we saw Dr Sensible on TV last night, your dad phoned her.
Dad I had to, son. She'll cure you.
Jimmy There's nothing to cure me of. I don't want the doctor's heartless medicine. Day-dreams are harmless. I can travel round the world in them, and do a million things we couldn't afford to do otherwise. Look around, Dad. Everything's grey here, and with birthdays gone it'll be worse. At least my day-dreams brighten things up.

Mum fusses at the table, laying breakfast bowls of cornflakes. Dad picks up the morning paper

Mum He could be right, Dad. Things do look a bit grey. Weren't things a teeny weeny bit more colourful once?
Dad What do you mean, Mum?
Mum Well, it seems the more famous Dr Sensible has become the greyer everything else has become. And I'm not sure I agree with you asking her to come here.
Jimmy You mean you asked her to come here!
Dad Yes, and it's too late to change our minds now. She'll be around in a . . .

The doorbell rings. Dr Sensible music

  Silhouetted against the glass panel is Dr Sensible. She seems to have horns

Jimmy It's the devil.
Dad I warned you about day-dr . . .

Dad looks up from his paper and sees the silhouette. The doorbell rings again, furiously, shaking the room. The family cower around the table as the door bangs open and Dr Sensible marches in, brisk, efficient, uptight and insane. She has a slight nervous tick which is evident when she has to mention any words like childhood or children. Behind her back she is holding a pitchfork, the prongs of which in silhouette have given the appearance of horns

Dr Sensible Who left this pitchfork in the garden? Leaving pitchforks in gardens is not very sensible.

She skewers a balloon with it, and will skewer other objects as well as threaten Jimmy

  And what are those flowers doing outside. They smell and attract ferocious butterflies. Petrol, I need some petrol. Quickly, man!

Dad, shell-shocked, points to a kitchen cupboard from which Dr Sensible takes a can of petrol

That's not a sensible place to leave petrol.

Dr Sensible marches to the door undoing the cap and tossing petrol on to the garden. She lights a match and throws it out. We hear a roaring noise and see flames and smoke. She slams the door

That's got rid of the flowers. Now, what's the problem here? Ah yes, a boy, (*she pokes Jimmy with the pitchfork*) small mucky boys are always a problem, 'specially small mucky boys who seem scared of nice sensible doctors. Come here, dwarf.

Jimmy is backed against the table by the pitchfork. She discards it, and opening her doctor's bag grabs him by the hair and begins to poke and examine him. Mum and Dad look on apprehensively

He hasn't got a cough, he hasn't got mumps, he hasn't got a chill, or any funny lumps. He hasn't got a tummy ache, he hasn't got a fever, he hasn't got a runny nose or chicken pox either. (*To Mum and Dad*) He doesn't look a ruin, he doesn't look a wreck, he hasn't got toothache, or a pain in the neck. He's fit as a fiddle, he's sound as a bell, I've never ever seen a boy looking so well.

Dad So tell us what's wrong.

Mum To know would be bliss.

Dr Sensible He's suffering from Dreamitis!

Mum ⎫
Dad ⎬ (*together, baffled*) Dreamitis?
      ⎭

Dr Sensible A condition caused by being young, not washing behind your ears, and writing poems.

She suddenly recoils from Jimmy, wiping her fingers as if he is contagious

Dreamitis!! It's impossible. He can't be suffering from Dreamitis. Every child in England is supposed to have taken my medicine and been cured. I must have missed him out. (*She threatens Jimmy*) Listen, shrimp, in exactly five days my medicine will be poured down the throats of every remaining child on the planet. But only on condition that every child in *this* country has taken it first. You, worm, are the only boy left in England not to have taken my medicine. (*Frantically worried*) If you haven't taken it by the deadline the whole lot will be poured away. (*Maniacally grabbing Jimmy and shaking him*) You must take my medicine before the deadline!

Jimmy I won't!

When Dr Sensible begins shaking Jimmy, Dad attempts, diplomatically, to restrain her. She bangs their heads together and they fall, dazed. From her bag she takes a flask and bottles. Mum and Dad assume frozen positions. Jimmy sits up and watches. Day-dream music. The Lights change slowly to lurid green. She prepares the medicine. Basic chemical illusions. It bubbles, it froths, it smokes. She dribbles

Dr Sensible Fieldmouse's pee and rattle-snake's spit,
A monkey's tongue (but only a bit)
Superglue and Bostik, kangaroo vomit

> Dog's turds and mole's fur
> With dead fleas on it.

(*Matter of factly*) Plus two aspirins and some Night Nurse. (*She pauses in her preparations*) This will rot his brain if nothing else does. That rebellious, mutinous, poetic spark will be snuffed out. (*She continues her preparations*)

> Snails crushed in pepper grinders,
> Fungus from a rat,
> A milky white eye from a very dead cat;
> Slime from the bottom of an old dustbin,
> Two little cockroaches crushed up thin.
> Juice from a cabbage boiled for a year,
> Squishy smelly wax from an old man's ear.

She rises from her preparations, holding a small phial of medicine up in triumph, laughing maniacally. Briskly she returns the things back to her bag. The Lights change back to "reality"

Oh, how I loathe children and their disobedient ways, and their revolting comics and stupid friendships. (*She bends down to Jimmy with the phial*) Drink this.

Jimmy refuses. Mum helps Dad to his feet

Mum (*whispering*) Are you sure you phoned the right doctor, dear?
Dad Positive, Mum. Maybe banging heads together's part of the cure.
Mum If you say so, Dad. Only I'm not convinced. I have my reservations about that doctor.

Jimmy gets up

Jimmy (*to the audience*) I think Dr Sensible's mad. I shouldn't take her medicine, should I? Right, I won't. I'll beat her deadline.

Dr Sensible puts her arms around the parents' shoulders conspiratorially

Dr Sensible See, he's talking to himself. A sure sign of Dreamitis. (*Slyly to Jimmy*) Go and make sure I've destroyed all those sickening flowers. And don't play with the cinders. I want a word with your mother and father alone. And no listening at the door.

Jimmy looks at Dad to see if he should go out. Dad nods

Jimmy leaves

Now then, (*she holds up the phial*) just one drop of this medicine is all that's needed to cure him. But, and this is a big *But*—it will only work if it is taken voluntarily. The trouble is, disobedient little children never take things voluntarily, so we'll have to get him to take it without him knowing, otherwise it won't work.
Dad Let me get this right. If we force Jimmy to take the medicine it won't work.
Dr Sensible Exactly.

Dad But if he doesn't know he's taken it, it will work?

Dr Sensible I'm glad you've got that into your thick head. We must put a drop into his food. That way it will work without him realizing he's taken it. Are these his cornflakes?

Mum and Dad nod, apprehensively

Dr Sensible Children are not very bright. There has never been one child in the history of the world who's outsmarted me. (*She pours a few drops of medicine on to the cornflakes*) There, done. Another childhood bites the dust!

Mum Are you sure it's the right amount, Doctor?

Dad Is there an antidote? I mean, if you give him too much can you reverse the process?

Dr Sensible That's easy. If you know how.

Mum }
Dad } (*together*) How?

Dr Sensible I've never revealed that secret to anyone. Now, call him back in, and remember, not a word about the medicine. He mustn't know it's in his cornflakes.

Dad Jimmy, come and get your breakfast.

Mum, Dad and Dr Sensible exit

Jimmy peers round the door, relieved that they've gone. He crosses to the breakfast table

Jimmy They've gone. Good. Maybe I can finally have my breakfast in peace.

He picks up his cornflakes and has the spoon near his lips before responding to the audience

What? She's put her medicine in my cornflakes? Which bowl? Are you sure? (*He puts the bowl down and picks up another one*) Has she put it in this bowl? Right, I'll have this one then. Where's the sugar? Mum's forgotten it again.

He goes off to get the sugar and Dr Sensible returns with Mum and Dad

Dr Sensible He's got the worst case of Dreamitis I've ever seen. I don't think I put enough medicine in his cornflakes. Now which bowl was his?

She adds medicine to a second bowl, making it two bowls now that contain the medicine

They exit as Jimmy returns with the sugar. The bowls will get so mixed up the audience won't know which one is which

Jimmy What? She's been at it again? Then which bowl of cornflakes can I eat? (*Swopping the bowls around*) This one? Or this one? Look, I think I'd better not eat anything while Dr Sensible's around. (*He picks up the paper*) Now, what's on TV tonight? Oh, good. The Invisible Man is on. You know, there's something that's always baffled me. I've always wondered why, when the Invisible Man eats his food, you can't see it rotting away in his stomach.

Day-dream music. If Jimmy recites rather than sings the poem, use "Intestine" music as background

Cousin Lesley took a pill
That made her go invisible.
Perhaps this would have been all right
If everything was out of sight.

But all around her stomach swam
Half-digested bread and jam
And no matter how she tried
She couldn't hide what was inside.

In the morning we often noted
How the toast and porridge floated
And how unappetizing in the light
Was the curry from last night.

Some old cheese had fallen victim
To her strange digestive system,
And there seemed a million ways
To digest old mayonnaise.

We were often fascinated
By the stuff left undigested,
A mishmash of peas and jelly
Slithered round our cousin's belly.

Certain bits of cornish pastie
Looked repugnant and quite nasty,
While the strawberries from last year
Were without the cream, I fear.

And at dinner, oh dear me!
What disgusting sight to see —
Chewed up fish and cold brown tea
Where Cousin Les's tum should be.

Dr Sensible enters. She looks very smug

Dr Sensible Another stupid poem. Well, that will be the last. In a few moments you'll hate poetry. You'll wonder why you ever bothered with the odious stuff.

Dr Sensible crosses to the table and consults the watch on her breast, then does a double take. She examines the whites of Jimmy's eyes. She picks up his bowl and sniffs it, then smashes it back down onto the table

Dr Sensible Imbecile! You've not eaten your cornflakes. You were spying at the door. Oh, you nasty, nasty little boy, spying.
Jimmy I wasn't spying. I was warned.

Dr Sensible Liar. Right, it's war. I'll find a way to pulverize your puerile fantasies. (*Unconsciously threatening him with a fork*) I'll find a ...

The doorbell rings. It is a very different ring from Dr Sensible's

Dad (*off*) See who it is, Jimmy.

Before Jimmy can open the door Mrs Scattybags, in all her glory, bursts in pushing a trolley. She might even have her invisible dog on a lead

Scattybags You-ee. It's me! I've escaped from the lunatic asylum—again!

Dr Sensible and Mrs Scattybags see each other simultaneously. Dr Sensible hisses and backs away horrified. Mrs Scattybags gasps, turns her trolley round, and clutching her hat does a full circle of the stage area, seeking a way out. She is constantly blocked by Dr Sensible, though the Doctor is likewise trying to avoid her

   Mrs Scattybags finally manages to get out

Dr Sensible I've caught Dreamitis. She wasn't real!
Jimmy That was my friend, Mrs——
Dr Sensible Scattybags?
Jimmy (*astonished*) You know her?
Dr Sensible (*hoarse*) Does she sometimes wear a hat with lobsters on it?
Jimmy Yes. It's always pinching things.
Dr Sensible Is she the kind of person who tickles babies under the chin?
Jimmy Very gently.
Dr Sensible Is she kind, warm, considerate, affectionate? The kind of person people want to (*as if it's a dirty word*) hug?
Jimmy Yes.
Dr Sensible Then that was my long lost twin sister! I had her put away in a lunatic asylum forty years ago.
Jimmy Oh, she's always escaping. But how can she be your twin sister?
Dr Sensible We looked alike to begin with, but the more sensible I became the more and more crazy she became.
Jimmy She writes great poems.

Jimmy goes and fetches one

Dr Sensible No!

The idea of a poem by Mrs Scattybags appeals to Dr Sensible as much as a cross to a vampire

   Not a Scattybags' poem! They're revolting!

Jimmy pursues Dr Sensible around the room, reciting the poem. The doctor can't stand it. It reduces her, briefly, to a nervous wreck

Jimmy   Pick-a-nose pick-a-nose pick-a-nose pick
                    Picked his nose and made me sick.
                    Pick-a-nose pick-a-nose pick-a-nose pick
                    Picks his nose very quick.

Pick-a-nose pick-a-nose pick-a-nose pick
Gets rid of it with one fast flick.
Flick flick flick flick flick
Pick-a-nose pick-a-nose makes me sick.

Dr Sensible manages to muffle the last "sick" with her hand over Jimmy's mouth

Dr Sensible It's the most disgusting thing ever written.

Dr Sensible, still muffling Jimmy, drags him over to the door and looks out

She's the only person in the world who knows the antidote to my medicine. Fortunately, she's so scatty she forgot it years ago.

Jimmy bites her hand and escapes. Dr Sensible hisses. The telephone rings. Dr Sensible snatches up the phone

This'll be the lunatic asylum wondering where Mrs Scattybags is (*On the phone*). Hallo, Lunatic Asylum? Mrs Scattybags has just been to Jimmy Smith's house. You're a load of loony nitbits letting her escape.

The Prime Minister appears, spotlight in separate area

Prime Minister I'm not a loony nitbit. I'm the Prime Minister. All that money the Government gave you to make your medicine work. Well, if it doesn't work on Jimmy Smith in five days we want our money back. Or you'll go to prison. We've sold lots of it to the President of the United States but he won't pay us for it if it doesn't work on Jimmy Smith.

Black-out. Spotlight in another area. A Reporter appears

Reporter This is Chuck Jones for CBS World News. Today the President of the United States discovered that Jimmy Smith is the only child left in Britain who has not taken Dr Sensible's medicine. Huge barrels of it are stored in warehouses throughout America, ready to be poured down the throats of every single child. But the President warned that unless Jimmy Smith takes it in five days all the medicine will be thrown away. "If Jimmy Smith doesn't take it, it can't be any good" is what he's saying.

The Second Reporter appears in another spotlight. The First Reporter waves at her but she pretends not to notice, being a little frosty

Second Reporter This is Pavlova Greshnichov from Russian Television News. In cities and villages all over Russia millions of children are urging Jimmy Smith to hold out for five days, otherwise they'll have to take the medicine as well and everything will turn grey and boring.

First Reporter School will last longer!

Second Reporter Children forgetting their gym gear will be *severely* punished.

First Reporter Playtime will be cancelled!

Second Reporter Ice creams outlawed!

First Reporter Sweets abolished!

The First Reporter exits

Second Reporter Cabbage compulsory!

The Second Reporter exits

Jimmy enters the spotlight

Jimmy Hamburgers illegal! Toys destroyed!

Fade spot in "reporter" area. Dr Sensible is looking at her watch in a panic

Dr Sensible Five days! Only five days! Take my medicine!
Jimmy No.
Dr Sensible How dare you defy me! I'll find a way to make you take it. (*She gathers up her bag*) And I'll be back sooner than you think.

Dr Sensible exits

Spot on Jimmy

Jimmy (*to the audience*) That was my first encounter with Dr Sensible, but it wasn't my last. Mum and Dad were as frightened of her as me, but they still trusted her, just because she was a doctor. Still, I only had to hold out for five days. Children all over the world were depending on me.

Jimmy exits

Fade to Black-out. Scene change music

SCENE 4

The kitchen. Next day

Mum, Dad and Jimmy enter

Jimmy (*to the audience*) Only four days left to hold out.

Dad and Jimmy sit at the table. Mum hovers over it laying breakfast

Mum All that kerfuffle yesterday. It exhausted me.

Dad picks up the paper and begins eating his breakfast. Jimmy takes an apple from his pocket

Dad It says here, Dr Sensible wants jelly to be banned immediately. She says it's the most dangerous substance in the world.
Jimmy (*astonished*) Jelly? Does the Government agree?
Dad Of course they'll agree.

Jimmy examines his apple with a large magnifying glass.

Mum Are you going to eat that apple, or are you just admiring it?
Jimmy I'm looking for pinpricks. Dr Sensible might have stuck a poisoned needle in it.
Mum But you guarded it all last night.

Jimmy I'm being extra vigilant. (*He sighs*) I do wish Mrs Scattybags was around to help. She's so scared of the doctor she's vanished.

Mum (*pulling Jimmy to her*) There, there. (*To Dad*) There's nothing wrong with the lad really, is there, Dad? (*Defiantly*) In fact, I quite like some of his poems. What's the one you wrote for me?

Jimmy   We love to squeeze bananas,
               We love to squeeze ripe plums,
               And when they are feeling sad
               We love to squeeze (*squeezing Mum*) our mums!

Mum That's the one.

A noise above them. Commotion music, a hint of "Jingle Bells". Somebody is having trouble on the roof

What's all that commotion up on the roof? It sounds like a herd of wild elephants.

Dad More like a kangaroo.

Soot and rubble clatters down the chimney and a boot appears. Mum investigates, tugging at the boot

Mum Give us a hand, you two.

Jimmy and Dad join in tug-of-war fashion. The boot comes off and they fall in a pile as Father Christmas comes crashing down the chimney followed by his sack. If the performance takes place any distance from Christmas, Father Christmas will be wearing a mixture of traditional and holiday gear ie, sunglasses and a loud shirt. This is really Dr Sensible in disguise

Father Christmas Ho ho ho. Happy Christmas all. Ho ho ho.

Father Christmas limps about and struggles back into his boot

Jimmy Wow! Father Christmas in our house. Christmas can't be banned.
Dad Fiddle. Of course it's banned.
Mum It did say so on TV . . .
Father Christmas Banned? Nonsense. Never heard such rubbish. I'll unban it immediately. (*Waving his hand*) When Father Christmas waves his hand, Jimmy's Christmas is unbanned.
Jimmy Hurray. How about my birthday? (*He dances around Father Christmas*)
Father Christmas That too.
Dad Hang on a minute. It's not Christmas yet.
Father Christmas Not Christmas? That's the trouble with these digital watches. Bang them against the side of an igloo and they speed up. Ah well, I'm here now/Anyway I'm here on my holidays.
Mum Shall I get a bowl of milk for your reindeer?
Father Christmas (*flustered*) Eh? What? Is it walrus milk? He only likes walrus milk.
Mum I'm afraid not. You can't buy walrus milk in Liverpool.

Jimmy tries to look in the sack, but Father Christmas slyly brushes him away

Dad I still think you've come too early.

Father Christmas It gets lonely in the North Pole with nothing to do except boss all my little dwarfs about. Ah well, I'm here now. (*Fishing in his sack*) This is for you, Dad. (*Giving him a rubber glove*) And for you, Mum. (*He gives her the other rubber glove or a few bricks*) And as for your charming little son—what would you like most in the world?

Jimmy To get rid of Dr S——

Father Christmas (*interrupting quickly*) How about a nice juicy hamburger for starters?

A brief burst of Dr Sensible music

Jimmy Great! (*He hesitates*) But . . . no . . . I'm being extra vigilant about my food.

Father Christmas With lashings of tomato ketchup and relish. Ah well . . .

Father Christmas is busy injecting medicine into the burger with an outsized hypodermic needle and acting shiftily

Jimmy I'll have it!

Jimmy takes the burger. He should be stopped from eating it by the children, who will have seen through Dr Sensible's Father Christmas disguise. If the warning is not forthcoming Dr Sensible can lift up the beard because it is itching. Jimmy flings the burger away. Dr Sensible snatches off her beard and flings it away

Dr Sensible How on earth could you possibly see through my brilliant disguise, you vile little boy?

Jimmy The children warned me.

Dr Sensible Warned you did they? And I suppose they shouted out "It's Dr Sensible."

Jimmy Yes, they did.

Dr Sensible Of course! There are hundreds of children here. They are scattered about everywhere. Dangling from the ceiling. Tap dancing round the room. Riding their bicycles up the walls. (*To Mum and Dad*) What a shame. I'm afraid his Dreamitis is out of control. Mum, Dad, can either of you see any children?

Mum and Dad look under chairs etc. Dad will be quicker than Mum to say no. The audience are likely to respond. Mum will listen, perhaps half hearing them. Then she'll decide "No"

Dad I can't see any kids.

Mum Unfortunately, I can't either.

Jimmy might have to calm the kids down, repeating that the grown-ups are unable to see or hear them because of having taken the medicine in their youth. Dr Sensible struggles out of her costume, looking far from sensible

Dr Sensible You should have taken my medicine at birth, that's when you should have taken it—when you were pink and wriggly and helpless.

Dad Oh come on, lad, take it and have done with it.

Jimmy (*adamant*) No!

Mum I can understand him not wanting to take it. It tastes a bit like pulverized frogs.

Dad I order you to take it!

Dr Sensible You can't order him. I've explained that. I'd order him to take it myself if it were possible. It's got to be taken voluntarily or without knowing, remember.

Jimmy I've got to hold out, Dad. For the sake of all the other children. She wants the world to be grey and boring. That's how you want it to be, isn't it, Dr Apprehensible? Mean and heartless like yourself.

Mum (*shocked*) Jimmy Smith!

Jimmy It's true. She's everything Mrs Scattybags isn't and she's jealous of the way children can have fun. I bet there are some people in England who haven't taken her medicine. (*He thinks about this*) I bet the Queen hasn't.

Slow lighting change. Feed in Dream music

Dr Sensible The Queen wouldn't need to take my medicine. She is a very sensible lady. And she has the most perfect manners in the entire world.

Either Mum or Dr Sensible act as the Queen. The others as attendants. In the first part of the poem/song the Queen is regal, and absurd in the second part

> I've never heard the Queen sneeze
> Or seen her blow her nose,
> I've never seen her pick a spot
> Or tread on someone's toes,
> I've never seen her slide upon
> A slippery piece of ice
> I've never seen her frown and say
> "This jelly is not nice."
> I've never seen her stick a finger
> In her royal and waxy ear,
> I've never seen her take it out
> And sniff, and say "Oh dear!"
> I've never seen her swop her jewels
> Or play frisbee with her crown,
> I've never seen her spill her soup
> Or drop porridge on her gown.

Jimmy
> Of course you haven't.
> But I wonder what she does
> When she sits at home alone,
> Playing with her corgies
> And throwing them a bone.
> I bet they've seen the Queen sneeze
> And seen her blow her nose,
> I bet they've seen her pick a spot
> And tread on someone's toes,
> I bet they've seen her slide upon

A slippery piece of ice,
I bet they've seen her frown and say
"This jelly is not nice."
I bet they've seen her stick a finger
In her royal and waxy ear,
I bet they've seen her take it out
And sniff, and say "Oh dear!"
I bet they've seen her swop her jewels
And play frisbee with her crown,
I bet they've seen her spill her soup
And drop porridge on her gown.
So why can't I do these things
Without being sent to bed,
Or failing that, why can't I
Be made the Queen instead?
Or the King at least.

Fade to Black-out. Bring up spots on empty stage area

*The Reporters, wearing reporters' macs, rush excitedly into the spots.
Chuck seems to have charmed Pavlova somehow. They wave to each other
and they've even swopped hats*

First Reporter Hallo, this is Chuck Jones from CBS World News again.

Second Reporter And this is Pavlova Greshnichov. A whole day has passed.

First Reporter Jimmy Smith now only has three days left to hold out against
taking Dr Sensible's medicine.

Second Reporter Dr Sensible is trying harder and harder to get him to take
it.

First Reporter She's injected it into a hard boiled egg.

Second Reporter She's sprinkled it on his chips.

First Reporter She's dropped it in his lemonade.

Second Reporter But Jimmy still hasn't taken it.

First Reporter In fact, he's now so scared he's stopped eating altogether.

Second Reporter He hasn't eaten a crumb for twenty-four hours.

First Reporter He only drinks tap water.

Second Reporter All over the world children are cheering him on.

First Reporter He's even written a new poem.

Second Reporter Run away run away run away quick.

First Reporter Dr Sensible's medicine makes me sick!

First Reporter   { *(together)* } Three cheers for Jimmy, three cheers for
Second Reporter { *(together)* } Jimmy. Hip-hip-hurrah, hip-hip-hurrah.

The Reporters exit, Jimmy enters the spot

Jimmy I was too clever for Dr Sensible until, when there were only two
nights to go, she played the meanest trick of all. I was weak with hunger,
and so tired that nothing could wake me up.

Fade to Black-out. Scene change music

SCENE 5

Jimmy's house. Night. The house is mouse-quiet

Dr Sensible enters through a window carrying her bag and wearing a burglar mask. Jimmy is in bed asleep

Dr Sensible I'll make him look like he's ill, then I can get him into my clinic, alone.

Dr Sensible tiptoes over to Jimmy's bed and opens her doctor's bag. She nearly knocks a lamp, or other object over, but saves it from falling. Then knocks it over again

Mum (*off*) I think I heard a noise downstairs, Dad.

Dr Sensible hides under the bed

Dad, in a nightgown, looks in the door. He shines a torch around, but sees nothing

Dad It's your imagination, Mum.

He exits

(*Off*) No-one here. Go back to sleep.

Dr Sensible gets out from under the bed. She takes a brush and make-up pots from her bag

Dr Sensible I'll make him look ill. A dab of green here.

Jimmy turns

(*She freezes*) A splodge of red dye there.

Jimmy turns again, she waits

Perfect. He looks chronic. He looks the sickest, measliest child in the world.

Dr Sensible crosses to the telephone and dials

And now for the most important part of my plan.

The telephone rings. Spot on the Prime Minister picking up the phone and also on Dr Sensible

Prime Minister Prime Minister here.

Dr Sensible Hallo, Prime Minister, this is Dr Sensible.

Prime Minister Has Jimmy Smith taken your medicine yet? I know it tastes like pulverized frogs, but that's no excuse. I'm being pestered by the President of the United States.

Dr Sensible Jimmy Smith is the most stubborn child in the world, but I've worked out a plan.

Prime Minister I should hope you have. If he hasn't taken it in two days you're for the chop. It'll be prison for you.

Dr Sensible I'm at his house now. There are blotches all over his face. Not only has he got Dreamitis, he's got the dreaded Morbillious Measles.

Prime Minister I've never heard of the dreaded Morbillious Measles, and I'm the Prime Minister.

Dr Sensible It's an absolutely new disease. Morbillious Measles is highly infectious. You must send an ambulance immediately. I want him taken to my clinic and put into isolation.

Prime Minister An ambulance is on the way.

Fade spot on Dr Sensible

Prime Minister Emergency! Emergency! Send an ambulance to Jimmy Smith's house immediately! Repeat, immediately. He has the dreaded Morbillious Measles! Repeat, the dreaded Morbillious Measles.

Fade spot. We hear the sound of sirens and the room is filled with flashing blue lights. (A strobe effect to give the sense of more people rushing around). Jimmy sits up

The door bursts open and men in frightening white costumes rush in

With cries of "Be careful", "He's deadly infectious", "He's got the dreaded Morbillious Measles", "Fumigate the room" etc. they strap him to a stretcher

Jimmy There's nothing wrong with me. Mum! Dad! Help me! I've never heard of Morbillious Measles. It's a trick. It's a trick.

Jimmy is taken struggling on the stretcher. The sirens and flashing blue lights fade

In the silence that follows Mrs Scattybags enters with her trolley. She looks around

Fade to Black-out

ACT II

Scene 1

Dr Sensible's Clinic

The sirens and flashing lights again. They fade as the excited Reporters dash on. Spot on Reporters. In the dimly lit background we see Dr Sensible's clinic. Jimmy is in a bed. We should have the visual sense of the clinic being surrounded by barbed wire. Whatever, Jimmy is isolated from the outside world. (Give the whole speech to the first Reporter if the second is needed to double as Dr Sensible's Assistant)

First Reporter Gosh, what exciting news! Jimmy Smith has been taken into Dr Sensible's private clinic after the doctor discovered he was suffering from the dreaded Morbillious Measles, an absolutely brand new disease that nobody has ever heard of except the wonderful Dr Sensible.

Second Reporter To stop the disease spreading, the entire clinic has been surrounded by soldiers all armed to the teeth. They are making quite sure nobody, absolutely nobody, can get in or out without special permission.

The Reporters exit

The Lights come up full as Dr Sensible enters pushing a body-sized trolley covered by a white sheet, beneath which there is definitely something. The sheet has a zip down the middle. She is followed by her mad Assistant pushing a smaller trolley on which there is a large platter and surgical instruments. Dr Sensible unzips the sheet. We cannot see what it is covering. Her actions will mask the operation. Jimmy peeps from under the bedcover. He'll strain to see what is happening with growing horror. Background sound of heart-beat

Dr Sensible Swab.
Assistant Swab.
Dr Sensible Tweezers.
Assistant Tweezers.
Dr Sensible Scalpel.
Assistant Scalpel.
Dr Sensible Hacksaw.
Assistant Hacks . . . oops! (*A clatter as she drops it*)
Dr Sensible Moron! It's all right. Stay calm. (*She aims a blow*)
Assistant (*ducking from Dr Sensible*) Moron!

The Assistant wipes Dr Sensible's forehead as she uses the hacksaw. From inside the cloth Dr Sensible lifts out what appears to be a small grey brain. She hands it to the Assistant who puts it on the platter. Jimmy watches, clutching his skull

Dr Sensible Tourniquet—quickly. Quickly! (*Pause*) Drill.
Assistant Drill.
Dr Sensible Clamp.
Assistant Clamp.
Dr Sensible Razor.
Assistant Razor.

Dr Sensible takes out a piece of raw liver and hands it to the Assistant who puts it on the platter

Dr Sensible Scraper.
Assistant Scraper.
Dr Sensible Pliers.
Assistant Pliers.
Dr Sensible Tongs.
Assistant Tongs.

Dr Sensible reaches her hand into the slit in the sheet and pulls out a roundish red object. Sound of a heartbeat stops as the Assistant puts this on the platter

Dr Sensible Syringe.
Assistant Syringe.
Dr Sensible Chisel.
Assistant Chisel.
Dr Sensible Knife.
Assistant Knife.
Dr Sensible Fork.
Assistant Fork.
Dr Sensible Salt.
Assistant Salt.
Dr Sensible Mustard.
Assistant Mustard.
Dr Sensible Pepper.
Assistant Pepper pepper. Peter Piper picked a peck of pepper.

Dr Sensible reaches into the sheet with both hands. She pulls out a piece of bloody liver, then brings out a soggy green mush and slaps it on to the platter. She should be rather strained by now. She lifts the sheet to wipe her hands and we see she has been preparing Jimmy's dinner. The Assistant places it on his bed

Dr Sensible Cauliflower, raw liver, beetroot and soggy sprouts. Try beating that for a sensible dinner. Eat.

Jimmy retires under the sheets making sounds of disgust

Assistant (*taking Dr Sensible aside*) Why don't you try and get him to eat something different, Doctor. Try and get him to eat some jelly.
Dr Sensible Jelly? (*She swipes at the Assistant*) Jelly's vile. It wobbles.

(*Another swipe*) Just thinking about the stuff makes me want to vomit. Never mention that word again.

Assistant But jelly is ——

Dr Sensible (*shrieking*) Don't mention jelly! I loathe every wobbly molecule of it. Out of my sight.

Dr Sensible takes a swipe at the Assistant who scurries to the door with the small trolley. Jimmy sees his chance to get rid of the food and scrapes it into the bedpan. The Assistant leaves and Dr Sensible turns her attention back to Jimmy. He burps, licks his lips and pats his tummy

Jimmy That was delicious.

Dr Sensible's nervous tick plays up on her as she stares at the plate. She's at a loss for what to say

Dr Sensible You've eaten it. Good. That's—well, that's very, very good. (*Nervous guttural laughter*) Now my medicine can be sold world-wide. (*She fiddles with the instruments on the trolley*) All those sweet brains anaesthetized. No more bright little faces with big wide eyes and wondrous expressions. No more childhood. No more day-dreams. I've saved the world from the scourge of happiness. Happiness! Ha! It's something I've never known, so why should a trillion chuckling children know it. (*In a panic*) I must inform the Prime Minister immediately. (*She picks up a surgical instrument and holds it to her ear*) Where's the phone, where's . . . (*Suddenly calming down*) You ate your dinner quickly.

Jimmy It was scrumptious, specially the raw liver.

Dr Sensible (*slyly*) Did the liver not taste a little, a touch, as it were, mediciney?

Jimmy Just a touch.

Dr Sensible flings the plate aside

Dr Sensible Perfidious worm! I injected the medicine into the sprouts, not the liver. (*Searching*) You're lying again, lying, what have you done with your dinner? Ha! Just as I thought!

She finds the bedpan and thrusts it towards him with a spoon

No? Starve then. (*She eats some herself*) You'll come crawling for food soon enough. When you're thin as a skeleton you won't be able to live on day-dreams and poetry. There's no escape from here, child.

Jimmy (*close to tears*) Mum and Dad will rescue me. I'll tell them you invented Morbillious Measles. Morbillious Measles don't exist!

Dr Sensible Who believes children? Children are physically incapable of telling the truth. Children are born with a mouthful of fibs. Their tongues are as twisted as corkscrews.

Jimmy Mum'll believe me.

Dr Sensible She won't even hear you. You're in isolation remember. Your parents have to stand behind that screen, and it's soundproof.

Jimmy You're a witch, not a doctor. You're . . .

Mum and Dad enter wearing surgical masks and protective clothes

Mum! Dad!

They do not hear Jimmy's cries for help. He scrambles from the bed. Dr Sensible hides the bedpan. On the other side of the "screen" Jimmy will try to mime his predicament, and Mum and Dad will misinterpret everything. Their noses and hands are up against the "screen"

Mum My poor little sweetheart. He looks excited to see us.

They wave

Dad Who'd have thought of it. (*Proudly*) Our lad the first person to catch the dreadful Morbillious Measles. He'll go down in medical history, Mum.
Mum Look Dad, he's rubbing his tummy.
Dad It must be all the fantastic grub he's getting here.
Mum And he is pointing down his mouth.
Dad He probably wants some sweets.

Jimmy has found a mop in the corner and uses it as a broomstick while pointing at Dr Sensible

Mum Now what's he doing that for?
Dad He's trying to tell us about all the fun and games he's playing with Dr Sensible. What a nice doctor.

Jimmy stirs witch's brew with the mop

Mum Look at his lips. I think he's saying something about witch's brew.
Dad No, Irish stew. I bet he eats plates of it here.

Jimmy gives up and flops on the bed exhausted

Mum (*dabbing her eyes*) Oh look, he's exhausted. Poor baby. (*Firmly*) I'm going to give him a hug. It's what mothers are for.

Dad holds her back, doing his solemn duty

Just one little motherly hug?
Dad Hugging's not allowed with Morbillious Measles, not even motherly hugs, it's far too infectious. Come on, Mum.

They mouth that they will come back tomorrow and make to exit. Mum pulls back and Jimmy regains hope

Mum I want to hug him. Hugging's in my blood!
Dad It's against the rules, Mum, and we have to obey the rules.

Music. The lights change

> Governments rule most countries,
> Bankers rule most banks,
> Captains rule their football teams
> And piranhas rule fish tanks.

There are rules for gnobling gnomes
And rules for frying frogs,
There are rules for biting bullies
And for vexing vicious dogs.

There are rules for driving motor cars
And crashing into chums,
There are rules for taking off your pants
And showing spotty bums.

There are rules for nasty children
Who tie bangers to old cats,
There are rules for running riot
And rules for burning bats.

There are rules in the classroom.
There are rules in the street.
Some rules are wild and woolly
And some are tame and neat.

And some are pretty sensible
And some are pretty daft;
Some I take quite seriously,
At others I have laughed,

But there is one special rule
You should not be without:
If you do not like the rules
OPEN YOUR MOUTH AND SHOUT!
OPEN YOUR MOUTH AND SHOUT!

Mum and Dad exit leaving:

Jimmy sitting dejected on the edge of his bed

The Lights fade to Black-out

SCENE 2

It is night in the Clinic. Jimmy is still sitting on the edge of his bed. There is a stronger sense of isolation—the shadow of barbed wire on the window, the distant voices of the guards. He gets up and tries the door and windows

Jimmy Locked. I'm trapped here. (*He looks at his watch*) The deadline's still not for ages. I've got to eat something even if it does have Dr Snideable's medicine hidden inside it. (*He sits hunched up on the bed, crying*) If only Mrs Scattybags was here, please God, send Mrs Scattybags.

A knock on the door and a rattle of keys

Mrs Scattybags?

But it is only the Assistant. She staggers in with a huge cake, dumps it on the trolley and switches on an extra light

Assistant That is the heaviest cake in the world. I don't know what Dr Sensible is up to having it delivered at this time of night.
Jimmy If it's from her, I don't want it.
Assistant Suit yourself. It was left outside my door with a note attached to it. (*She shows him the note*) "Take this to Jimmy at once, or else." Signed Dr Sensible.
Jimmy It's probably covered in her special medicine.
Assistant (*as she goes*) Naturally.

The Assistant exits

Jimmy turns his back on the cake, resolutely. The top of the cake moves slightly. When the children tell him, Jimmy will turn, see nothing, and turn away again, disinterested. The top of the cake moves again. A hand reaches out, feels about, and plucks a cherry from the top of the cake before disappearing back inside. Jimmy turns and spots a movement. As he walks cautiously towards the cake, the top rises and, simultaneously, there is a brief burst of suitable fun-fair music and whirling lights, as Mrs Scattybags rises up out of the cake, revealing the top to be her hat. Jimmy and Mrs Scattybags whirl about and hug

Jimmy Mrs Scattybags! I knew you wouldn't let me down.
Scattybags Hush. Dr Sensible's sleeping next door. When I saw her in your house I guessed right away what she was up to. It's wicked the way she's turned out, that's what it is—wicked and sanctimonious. But we've got to get you out of here. Quickly, into the cake.

Jimmy walks over to the cake

Jimmy She said there's a secret antidote to her medicine, only you've forgotten it.
Scattybags It's something to do with . . . but no, I have forgotten it. Quickly now, into the cake.
Dr Sensible (*off*) What's that noise?
Scattybags Hurry.

Jimmy sinks into the cake. Mrs Scattybags arranges pillows and a mop to give the appearance of Jimmy in bed

Scattybags (*in a tither*) Oh the shame of it, the shame. Such a terrible sister.

Mrs Scattybags is putting on a surgical mask as the keys rattle in the door. She realizes she is still wearing the top of the cake as a hat, and just manages to get it on to the cake as:

Dr Sensible, dressed in her nightgown, enters. She looks at the bed, then sees Mrs Scattybags who is standing with her back to the cake

Dr Sensible You're not my assistant.
Scattybags (*inspired*) I'm your assistant's assistant.
Dr Sensible No you're not. My assistant's assistant is on holiday.

Scattybags I mean I'm your assistant's assistant's assistant.

Dr Sensible I don't think I believe you.

Scattybags You are absolutely right. I'm really only your assistant's assistant's assistant's assistant. I'm so keen to follow in your footsteps I'm practising on this wicked child.

Dr Sensible Don't I know you? You look familiar ... You're not ...? No, impossible. (*She spots the cake*) And what's this?

Scattybags I thought we might sprinkle a little of your wonderful medicine on it.

Dr Sensible I've better plans. Take it away. And you're fired.

Dr Sensible makes as if to lift a sheet on the bed and look at Jimmy. Instead she studies his progress chart. Mrs Scattybags pushes the trolley towards the door

Jimmy (*from inside the cake*) I've got cramp.

Dr Sensible (*turning*) What?

Scattybags I've got damp—I mean sweaty, from lifting the cake.

Dr Sensible Oh, get out. (*She turns back to the chart*)

Scattybags (*to Jimmy*) Hush.

Dr Sensible turns back again

Push. I can't push the door open.

Dr Sensible (*opening the door*) You pull it, not push it, idiot!

Mrs Scattybags is half way through the door with the cake. Dr Sensible pinches the back of her dress with her finger and thumb and pulls her back into the room

Wait. Leave that ridiculous cake alone.

Mrs Scattybags frowns. Dr Sensible reaches for her surgical mask

Let me see your face.

Mrs Scattybags tries to back away but the mask is pulled from her

You!

Scattybags Yes, me, Mrs Scattybags, you inhuman monster! Look out, behind you!

Dr Sensible falls for the ruse. Mrs Scattybags grabs a hypodermic needle from the trolley and jabs her in the behind. A terrible fight ensues, in which all manner of things can be used: walking sticks as swords, surgical instruments, tweezers, pillows, artificial limbs from a cupboard—even a cylinder of laughing gas could come into play. Jimmy comes out of the cake and provides the final blow. It is not all a panto fight—quite a violent affair. Violent words are exchanged, i.e.

Scattybags Take that, quack!

Dr Sensible And you take that, loon!

Scattybags And that, heartless blackguard!

Dr Sensible I'll knock some sense into you.

Scattybags And I'll knock it out of you, fiend!

Dr Sensible Screwball.

Scattybags Hypocritical oaf, dehumanized dream-killer!

Dr Sensible I'll rip out your liver, I'll unwind your intestines!

Scattybags That's for being sensible. And that's for being mean to children, and that's—oh that's for being you.

Dr Sensible receives a stunning blow

Mrs Scattybags and Jimmy make their escape

Dr Sensible Escaped! It's not sensible. It's ... Oh, I'll track those rebels down. I'll have her locked away in the deepest, darkest, slimiest asylum. I'll have her locked away until the clothes rot from her body!

Dr Sensible is raging, shaking her fist at the gods

And him, I'll subtract the day-dreams from his soul and drown them like kittens. I'll follow him to the ends of the earth. That mutinous, that insubordinate, that undisciplined and traitorous child!

Black-out

Spot on Reporter. He's breathless with excitement

First Reporter Hallo. It's Chuck Jones from CBS World News again. We've just received some amazing information. Dr Sensible's been knocked senseless. Kapow! Wham! Splat! And Jimmy's escaped. Yes folks, escaped with the help of Mavis Scattybags, the forgetful batty scag lady, er, scatty bag lady. Gosh, I'm tongue tied with excitement. The Prime Minister is double furious with Dr Sensible. "All that money we gave her to make her medicine. Well, we want it back or she'll go to prison" is what the PM's saying. Mums and dads all over England are beginning to wonder if the medicine is so good after all. And in America the President is still grumbling, "The medicine can't be any good if Dr Sensible can't get Jimmy to take it". The plucky lad's mum and dad have received over a million letters, all begging Jimmy to hold out. Less than three hours to go before the deadline! And nobody knows where Jimmy is. The army's looking for him! The police are looking for him, everyone's looking for Jimmy. Especially Dr Sensible. She is searching the city at this very moment.

The Reporter exits

Black-out. Scene change music

SCENE 3

The city at night. A grey, deserted place. Derelict tower blocks and evidence of what was once a thriving community. In gaping windows can be seen torn curtains. Bits of junk, litter and a few dustbins on stage

Jimmy and Mrs Scattybags are walking hurriedly through the cold night, looking fearfully over their shoulders. Mrs Scattybags, in essence a bag lady, is pushing a trolley full of junk. Occasionally she will find something—a boot, a can, whatever, and adds it to the trolley. They are a bit out of breath

Scattybags This was a lovely place once, Jimmy. But that was before Dr Sensible's medicine came along. Oh, that vindictive woman! Who'd have guessed we were born twins! You know, Jimmy, in everyone there're good bits and bad bits, but when we were born she got all the bad bits and I got all the good bits.

Jimmy What's in the trolley, Mrs Scattybags? (*He investigates*)

Scattybags All my bits and pieces.

Jimmy But no food?

Scattybags Not a crumb.

Jimmy I'm *so* hungry and cold. I'll have to give in to her before I starve to death.

Scattybags Give in? Not while there's an itchy witchy bit of a dream inside you. Give in indeed! To Dr Sensible? Never! What about all those children who are relying on you?

Jimmy But ...

Scattybags After all the wickedness she's done. She gave her medicine to your mum and dad when they were little, didn't she?

Jimmy Yes.

Scattybags And what are they like now? All the nice fun things your dad wanted to do—did he do any of them?

Jimmy shakes his head

And your poor mother—has she ever had any fun?

Jimmy (*faintly*) No.

Scattybags Then cross your heart and promise me you won't give in.

Jimmy I promise and ...

Dr Sensible music

In one of the tenement windows we suddenly see Dr Sensible's head. It should catch the audience by surprise and shock them as much as it does Jimmy and Mrs Scattybags

Dr Sensible (*off*) He's here somewhere. I can sniff out rebellious children. Police! Get a move on!

Sirens and flashing lights. Jimmy and Mrs Scattybags hide in the dustbins as:

Dr Sensible, hypodermic needle at the ready, enters at the same time as the Policeman. For a heart-stopping moment, it looks as if Jimmy and Mrs Scattybags will be discovered

We must find that child soon. And don't you go wasting your time helping little old men across the road. And throw that chewing gum into a bin!

The Policeman takes out his gum, lifts Mrs Scattybags' bin-lid and throws it in. As he turns away it is thrown out again

(*Spotting the gum*) I said into a bin, not on the ground.

The Policeman throws it into Jimmy's bin and it is thrown out again, unseen by him. On both occasions the audience should feel Jimmy and Scattybags are in danger of being caught

Now, let's go and search.

As they exit in different directions the Policeman spots the gum, shrugs and slyly pops it back into his mouth

Jimmy and Mrs Scattybags rise from their bins, covered in fish-bones etc

Jimmy Where can we hide?
Scattybags (*standing*) I know a safe place. But we have to pass through the Forbidden Zone.
Jimmy It sounds scarey.
Scattybags The Forbidden Zone's more stupid than frightening. Come on, Jimmy, and stay close.

Fade Lights. Music. The Lights change

A huge moon is rising, behind the city scape. If using gauzes, feed in lights that will show the Forbidden Zone, which will bring into vision notices saying "Keep Off!" "Do Not Enter!" "No Exit!" etc. Jimmy is lagging behind Mrs Scattybags. He picks up a decaying notice-board

Jimmy It looks harmless enough here.
Scattybags I did say it was a more stupid than frightening place. Dr Sensible put these signs up when she was younger. In those days all she wanted to do was ban everything.

Jimmy takes out a hanky and begins to clean up the notice-board

Jimmy (*reading*) "The For-bid——(*he cleans some more*) en zone." It's forbidden to walk on the grass. It's forbidden to stand still. It's forbidden to move . . . It's just like being at home this. It's forbidden to do anything.
Dad (*off*) Jimmy! Jimmy!
Jimmy Mrs Scattybags, I think I can hear someone calling.
Scattybags (*exiting*) Come on, Jimmy, no dawdling, love. We've a long way to go.

Mrs Scattybags exits

Jimmy I'm sure I can hear someone. Maybe not.

Jimmy drops the notice-board and follows after Mrs Scattybags. As he exits we hear Dad again

Dad (*off*) Jimmy, Jimmy!

Dad enters. He is wearing a grey overcoat and a grey scarf

Where on earth is the lad? And where, for that matter, am I? (*He picks up the notice-board and reads it*) "The Forbidden Zone". I wish I could find our Jimmy. I'll never forgive myself for letting Dr Sensible take him away. I'll get Mum, and we'll carry on looking for him together. Jimmy! Jimmy!

Dad exits, dejected. Jimmy enters, having lost Mrs Scattybags

Jimmy (*whispering*) Mrs Scattybags, Mrs Scattybags?

The Policeman enters

Policeman Oi! You! Whatcha up to?

Jimmy is flustered. He puts on a pair of shades, trying to disguise himself

Jimmy I've lost a friend.
Policeman Have you now? It's forbidden to lose people here. This is the Forbidden Zone.
Jimmy But if I look for my friend I'll find her.
Policeman It's also forbidden to find people.
Jimmy But I'll feel sad if I don't find her.
Policeman Oi! Feeling sad's forbidden.
Jimmy Good. If I find her I'll feel happy.
Policeman Feeling happy's 'specially forbidden. You've broken the rules. I'm taking you to prison. (*He takes out a pair of handcuffs; dithers*) The trouble is, as everything is forbidden it's also forbidden to take people to prison.
Jimmy Is there anything that's not forbidden here?
Policeman I'm forbidden to tell you.
Jimmy Why?
Policeman I'm forbidden to tell you why I'm forbidden to tell you.
Jimmy The Forbidden Zone's daft. I've never heard of anywhere as dumb as this place.
Policeman Oh, I agree.
Jimmy You agree?
Policeman Certainly. It's forbidden to disagree. If it wasn't forbidden to disagree I don't know what I'd think because thinking's forbidden, you see.
Jimmy (*getting a bright idea*) Is it forbidden for me to tweak your nose?
Policeman Oh, certainly.
Jimmy Is it forbidden for me *not* to tweak your nose?
Policeman Er . . . yes, that's forbidden as well.
Jimmy Then I better had.

Jimmy tweaks the Policeman's nose while he stands rigid, suffering

How about chinese burns?
Policeman It's forbidden to give policemen chinese burns.
Jimmy I suppose it's also forbidden *not* to give policemen chinese burns?
Policeman Yes . . .

Jimmy gives the Policeman a chinese burn

Jimmy How about kicking policemen in the bum. Is it forbidden *not* to kick policemen in the bum?
Policeman Of course it is. (*Puffed up*) I am a policeman.
Jimmy Oh, dear. I'd better obey the rules.

Jimmy kicks the Policeman in the bum

Policeman (*he's had enough*) And it's 'specially forbidden not to clobber little smart alecs.

Jimmy dodges the Policeman who chases him off

Mum and Dad enter. Dad is comforting Mum. She is wearing a grey coat and is carrying a shopping bag

Mum (*drying her tears*) I'm fed up with Dr Sensible. Sometimes I'd like to ... I'd like to ... to do something *not* sensible!!
Dad Let's try then!
Mum Oh yes! Bother Dr Sensible! Remember in the days before we took her medicine—that dance we did?
Dad The Wobbly Bum and Custard Pie Dance?
Mum The very dance. We did it when we were young.
Dad When we were happy.
Mum When we first fell in love.
Dad Before we were sensible.
Mum Let's do it again. Now. Oh, I'm so excited.
Dad Have you any custard pies in your shopping bag?
Mum Two.
Dad Two! Exactly the number we need!
Mum Can you really remember the dance?
Dad Yes. And you?
Mum Yes!

A brief pause in their excitement

Dad Are you sure we should?
Mum In the Forbidden Zone?
Mum ⎫
Dad ⎭ (*together*) Yes! Let's do it then.

Music

The Wobbly Bum and Custard Pie Dance is a cross between a tango and flamenco, with a bit of martial arts and a touch of ballroom dancing thrown in, solemnly silly. When bums are bumped together the custard pies nearly go in the holder's own face. There is the expectancy that they will pie each other because of their ridiculous movements. It is vaudeville stuff

The dance is interrupted by the Policeman who enters looking worse for wear from Jimmy's tweaks and kicks

Policeman Oi! You can't do that!

The dance music winds to a halt. Mum and Dad close up together

Mum We're enjoying ourselves. Like we did when we were young.
Dad When we were happy.
Policeman This is the place Dr Sensible first had the idea for her glorious

medicine. It's forbidden to be happy here. Er ... it's also forbidden to tweak and kick policemen.

Mum We'd never do a thing like that, would we, Dad?

Dad No. We were dancing to cheer ourselves up.

Mum Yes. We felt miserable. We can't find our Jimmy.

Policeman Nor can I.

Mum You mean you're looking for our Jimmy? You're chasing my harmless little lamb?

Dad (*starting up the dance again*) Are we forbidden not to shove these custard pies in your face?

Policeman You are absolutely forbidden not to ... Oh no, I hate this job. I want my mummy!

Mum } (*together*) { Policeman pie, policeman pie, shove it down his trousers
Dad } { and make him cry.

The Policeman stands blubbering as the pies are applied. Mum takes a large dummy from her shopping bag and sticks it in his mouth

Mum and Dad rush off, taking some of the signs with them, chased by the Policeman

Policeman (*exiting*) Stop, go, halt, move away, come back!

The Lights cross-fade as:

Jimmy and Mrs Scattybags enter

Jimmy I'm sure I heard Dad around here somewhere. I feel weak with hunger, Mrs Scattybags.

Scattybags There's not long to hold out now.

Jimmy I don't care, I feel ...

Jimmy collapses

Scattybags (*rushing to his aid*) Fainted. If only there was some food Dr Sensible hasn't contaminated.

A hand bell is heard ringing, off

Scattybags (*sniffing*) What's that delicious smell? It's chips!

Jimmy (*bolting upright*) And sizzly sausages!

Scattybags And fish fingers.

Jimmy And hot doughnuts!

Scattybags And cakes and gingerbread.

Jimmy And—look!

A burst of bright fair-ground music as a food stall is wheeled on to the stage by Dr Sensible disguised as Antonio. It is decked out in fairylights and looks a bit like a Punch and Judy stall, only decorated with images of food. Antonio is singing something daftly operatic. He opens the shutters

Jimmy and Mrs Scattybags wander mesmerized and salivating towards him

Antonio Ah, it is Jimmy and the lovely Mrs Scattybags. Welcome, welcome!

I kissa you both on the cheeks. (*He does so*) People are stupida. There are no Morbillious Measles.

Jimmy wipes his cheeks, hating grown-up kisses. Mrs Scattybags simpers at the handsome Antonio

You both looka hungry. You are a-missing the food?

Mrs Scattybags suddenly remembers something and whispers in Jimmy's ear. He looks crestfallen

Scattybags I'm afraid we have a problem, Mr, er ——
Antonio Call me Antonio.
Jimmy Mrs Scattybags has got no money.
Scattybags (*sighing*) I seem to forget so many things.
Antonio For Jimmy and the beautiful Mrs Scattybags no money is a-wanting.

Antonio returns to the stall and takes out a folding table and chairs which he sets up with a cloth and candles etc. He will appear to produce food from thin air as well as the stall

Let Antonio giva you the feast of your lives. To begin, giant hamburgers made with whole cow, all a-tasty and a-calorific. And the angel cake made for (*he looks at Mrs Scattybags*) an angel.

Mrs Scattybags, true to habit, secretes some away in her trolley. She tucks into the food

Jimmy goes to eat then hesitates

Jimmy (*a sudden realization*) What time is it?

Mrs Scattybags reaches over and takes an alarm clock from the trolley

Scattybags (*hyper-excited*) It's nearly dawn, why, Jimmy, bless you, you've done it! You've beaten Dr Sensible! Only five minutes to go before the deadline. How wonderful! We'll be free of Dr Sensible at last!

Mrs Scattybags flings food about with excitement. Antonio picks it up and replaces it

Jimmy I'd better wait those five minutes.
Scattybags Surely there's no need?
Antonio You breaka Antonio's heart, not a-wanting my food.
Jimmy I do. But I'll wait. There's only a few minutes now.

Antonio piles the food up in front of Jimmy

Antonio OK you waita; but now Antonio is too sad to read his poem. (*He wipes away crocodile tears with a cloth which is over his arm*)
Jimmy Hey! You write poems as well.
Antonio I, Antonio Michaelangelo writa poems? At school I was always doing the day-dream and a writing the poem—eata hamburger.

Jimmy absentmindedly picks up the hamburger. Antonio is encouraged by this, but Jimmy doesn't eat it

You have the poem about a little sister? I tell you a crazy poem abouta Milkshake Cafe I used to have. Then may-bea you eat. Music! Lights!

Music. The Lights change. Antonio sings or recites "The Milk-shake Cafe". Jimmy is continually about to eat the hamburger but doesn't

Jimmy   } *(together)*
Mrs Scattybags }

I went in to the milk-shake cafe
And saw the milk-shake cows,
They stood behind the counter
In different flavoured rows.

The banana-flavoured milk-shake cow
Ate bananas by the bunch,
The strawberry-flavoured milk-shake cow
Had strawberries for lunch.

The lemon-flavoured milk-shake cow
Sulked and spat out pips,
The orange-flavoured milk-shake cow
Had orange coloured lips.

Antonio

To get the milk-shake frothy
There was a strange machine
It milked the mooing cows
And turned their milk to cream

There were so many different flavours
We were spoilt for choice
Until one day the owner said
In a trembly sort of voice

Quick! Clear out the cafe,
I've just been told today
The place is being raided
By the RSPCA.

Scattybags (*finishing a doughnut*) Divine! You're a bright light in a dark, sensible world, Mr Antonio.

Antonio You both a make me very happy. Now have some sweets.

They take some

Filla your pockets.

Jimmy (*excited by this idea*) Why not give some to the children? (*To the audience*) Would you like some? (*To Antonio*) You can see them, can't you Antonio? It's only boring old sensible groanups who can't.

Antonio I giva the sweets to the beautiful children in their pretty pink party frocks.

Mrs Scattybags is slapping on make-up with the aid of a vanity mirror while Antonio throws sweets everywhere except to the audience

Jimmy No, Antonio. They're over there.
Antonio You eata your hamburger. I needa my glasses.

As Antonio returns to the stall, Jimmy eats his hamburger

Jimmy (*frowning*) This hamburger tastes funny.
Scattybags And so do these sweets, they taste a bit like ——
Jimmy Squidgy toads?
Scattybags Boiled mice? They taste like ——
Jimmy Dr Sensible's medicine!!

They spit the sweets and hamburger out. Jimmy grabs the clock. A moment's silence. Mrs Scattybags waits in horror

There's still three seconds to go . . .

From behind the stall Antonio snatches off a wig and false moustache, triumphantly revealing himself as Dr Sensible

Dr Sensible They taste like my medicine because that's what they're full of.
(*Manic laughter*) It was also in the hamburgers. It was in everything!
You've stuffed yourself full of sensible medicine. I used the most acrid
fieldmouse's pee; the squidgiest frogs; the most succulent boiled mice, and
several ingredients too disgusting to mention. I've triumphed!
Scattybags (*in a moment of revelation*) You are mad. You've fooled
everyone into believing you're sane. But you're so sane you're . . . oh,
cruelly mad.

*Mrs Scattybags guides Jimmy behind her protecting him with her bulk. He is
trying to vomit. As Dr Sensible speaks she is closing up her stall. The
brightness and colourfulness of the scene is fading and the world is becoming
grey again*

Dr Sensible (*to Mrs Scattybags*) You're too scatty for my medicine to work
on. (*To Jimmy*) But you . . . it'll begin soon. You'll feel a tightness in your
throat, your belly will ache—and then, you'll forget your silly rhymes.
You'll hate them. (*She begins to push the stall off*) Fun! You'll shudder at
the word. Laughter! It will sound like the braying of a mule. Happiness!
Oh you'll feel bitter and mean at the thought of it ever existing.
Scattybags "Bitter at the thought of happiness existing!" That describes her
exactly. Oh you . . . you . . . oh, the shame of it. You as a sister!
Dr Sensible And if I felt anything for you it would be pity. You're so feeble-
brained you can't remember a simple antidote. (*She throws a bundle on to
the stage*) Here, child. These are sensible clothes. I'll leave them behind for
you.

Dr Sensible exits

Mrs Scattybags hurries after her flinging a suitable object from the trolley

Jimmy is slumped on the ground, disinterested

Scattybags (*urgently*) Oh my poor brain. It's crowded with so much junk I
can't sift through it. What is the antidote? Let me think. (*She sees Jimmy*)

No! You mustn't just sit there. (*Getting him to his feet*) You must fight against the medicine.

Jimmy shakes his head

Yes. Fill your head with day-dreams. Oh Jimmy, there are times to be sensible, but not now. What she wants is for you to be unhappy, and mean, and lonely. Like her.

Jimmy pulls away from Mrs Scattybags and wanders over to the bundle of clothes from which he takes a "sensible" coat and wears it instead of his bomber jacket. He tries on sensible shoes. From now on for Jimmy it is a struggle. His voice and manner will alternate between his own and a voice and manner that is horribly cold and "sensible"

Jimmy (*trying on the shoes*) These look more sensible than my trainers.
Scattybags (*to the audience*) He's going to become like that putrid woman. What can I do? Shall I try and tell him a few jokes? Jokes aren't sensible. They might slow the medicine down. Jimmy, what wobbles when it flies?
Jimmy Eh?
Scattybags A jellycopter!

Jimmy doesn't even smile

Scattybags It's no use. I'll try a few funny poems. "The Giant's Dinner". For dinner I ate a little boy, he tasted really funny. I spat him out right away because his nose was runny!

No response from Jimmy

What's another? The Invisible Man's Invisible Dog! My invisible dog is not much fun. I don't know if he's sad or glum. I don't know if, when I pat his head, I'm really patting his bum instead.

A weak smile from Jimmy

Jimmy I don't like the feeling of this medicine, Mrs Scattybags. I'm scared. No, I'm not, I feel quite sensible.
Scattybags It's getting worse. He's splitting up into two people. (*She grabs Jimmy by the arms*) Listen Jimmy, I'm your friend, aren't I?
Jimmy No. (*With effort*) Yes.
Scattybags And you still want to have fun and be happy?
Jimmy It's not sens ——
Scattybags Say yes.
Jimmy Yes.
Scattybags And you still want to hug your mum when she's sad.
Jimmy No. Sometimes I feel like part of the furniture in our house—as if by having me it completed the family, like a TV set or a fridge.
Scattybags Shame on you, Jimmy Smith! They love you.

Jimmy does not respond

That vile medicine is making you heartless. If only I could remember the antidote. It was something that Dr Sensible . . . that she . . . oh bother. I can't remember.

Jimmy I'm beginning to feel cold inside. I'm beginning to hate the things I loved. Mrs Scattybags, I'm going to Dr Sensible's clinic. Maybe I can find the antidote there.

Scattybags (*in a panic*) We'll go together. We'll . . . we'll bash her!

Jimmy No, I'll go alone.

Scattybags Hurry then. You haven't a moment to lose. I'll find your mum and dad and explain everything. Hurry Jimmy. Hurry before the medicine overpowers you completely.

They exit in different directions

Scene change music

SCENE 4

Dr Sensible's Clinic

Jimmy is in the Clinic, shining his torch. We are back at the opening scene

Jimmy Well, that's the story so far. That's how I came to be here.

The Light Jimmy is standing in is slowly turning him grey. A shudder runs through him

The medicine's really working now. You are fading, like ghosts. (*To himself*) Maybe Dr Sensible was right after all. Maybe I'm just imagining there are children here. (*Shouting as if to an empty auditorium*) Is anyone there? (*In a serious voice*) Oh, this is absolutely dumb. What's this? (*He fishes in his pocket and takes out a catapult or waterpistol*) A stupid, childish toy. (*He throws it away*) How could I ever have been amused by such rubbish.

Dr Sensible music. The sound of manic laughter as in the opening scene. Dr Sensible appears, silhouetted like something from a vampire movie

Dr Sensible Boy?

Jimmy (*staring ahead, not turning*) Yes, Doctor?

Dr Sensible Who were you talking to?

Jimmy No-one. I was imagining things.

Dr Sensible Tell me a poem.

Jimmy I can't remember any.

Dr Sensible A joke?

Jimmy I've forgotten them all.

Dr Sensible Can you see any children anywhere?

Jimmy No.

Dr Sensible Or smell them?

Jimmy No.

Dr Sensible And now for the final test. Do you like jelly?

Jimmy No.

Dr Sensible Perfect. You are obviously cured. Jelly. How I loathe that disgusting wobbly stuff. It's the thing I hate most in the world. Now I'll phone the Prime Minister and let him know you've taken my medicine. At last it can be released worldwide, (*She picks up the phone and begins dialling*)

Mrs Scattybags bursts onto the stage pushing her trolley with Dad in tow

(*Hissing*) You!

Scattybags Yes, me! I've told your dad everything, Jimmy.

Dad (*to Dr Sensible*) If I'd have known how nasty you were I would never have let you near our Jimmy.

Scattybags That's the spirit, Dad. You tell her! Did you find the antidote, Jimmy?

Mrs Scattybags rushes towards him. Jimmy flinches and pushes her away in distaste

Jimmy Keep your distance, old woman. To imagine I could have loved someone as ragged as you. What a stupid, shabby person you are. A dismal failure. Away with you.

Mrs Scattybags stops in horror, frozen. Dad also loses his certainty. Dr Sensible preens

Dad Show a little kindness, son. Scatty's part of the family. She loves you.

Jimmy So? Is there a law saying I must love her back. Love is not sensible Father.

Dr Sensible Well said, child. (*To Mrs Scattybags*) Take that stupid trolley away from here. You are not wanted.

Scattybags Jimmy . . .

Jimmy Go away. Take her away, Father.

Dad You've really taken the medicine.

Jimmy It's what you wanted.

Dad Yes. No. Oh, I'm a warren of confusion.

Jimmy Just get rid of her. See, she's slobbering now.

Mrs Scattybags is sobbing, wringing her hankie. Dad takes her gently by the elbow and leads her to the edge of the stage area. The trolley stays on stage. Follow spot on Mrs Scattybags as she makes for the auditorium exit

Scattybags It's all my fault. I'm a useless old thing. If only I could remember what the antidote was. Now no-one will love me, not one single child. (*To the audience*) I'm sorry I couldn't remember the antidote. Do you forgive me? Will anyone forgive me? Oh, thank you! The only thing I remember about the antidote is that it's something Dr Sensible hates, something she hates most in the world. What? What does she hate most? Jelly? That's it, that's the antidote! How could I have forgotten. It's gargling with jelly!!

Mrs Scattybags rushes back on to the stage. She rummages in her trolley flinging out a flipper and a football boot amongst other things. She finds a rusty old blunderbuss and tosses it to Dad

Cover her, Dad. I'm sure I had a few lumps of jelly at the bottom of this trolley. Yes, I have. Now where's my flask of scalding tea?

Dr Sensible tries to edge away but Dad does not let her. Mrs Scattybags puts the jelly in the flask and shakes it

It's far too hot.

She cools her mixture with water from a jug somewhere in the clinic

That should cool it down nicely. (*She gargles*) Yuck. Tea-tasting jelly. Quick Jimmy, gargle before it sets. It's impossible to gargle with jelly once it's set.

Jimmy I don't want to. It's not sensible.

Dr Sensible (*to Mrs Scattybags*) The child is right, it's perfectly absurd. (*To Dad*) How dare you point a gun at me.

She steps towards Dad but he is not going to be intimidated

Dad Jimmy, I order you to gargle with that jelly. If you are sensible, you'll do what you are told.

Jimmy refuses

(*Yelling; angry*) Do it!

Jimmy takes the flask and gargles. The stage is brighter. It begins to fill with colour and will continue to do so as the others gargle

Jimmy Wow! I feel like me again. (*He realizes he has a sensible coat on and takes it off*) Yuck.

Scattybags Now give her some. Give her lots.

Jimmy My pleasure.

Dr Sensible I refuse. I loathe jelly. It shudders. It wobbles!

Dr Sensible makes to bolt but Mrs Scattybags, armed with perhaps a yellow duck water-ring and a funnel from the trolley overpowers and sits on her

Scattybags Refuse, do you? Come on Jimmy.

The funnel is held to her mouth and Jimmy pours the jelly down it

Gargle, witch. Oh, I haven't had such fun for a long time. This'll teach you to be cruel and mean to children.

Dr Sensible staggers to her feet. More lights sparkle. Woozy, she stumbles out of the door. (Or if we can have the "transformation" on stage so much the better)

Oh dear me, I think we got carried away. It's jelly potent stuff this. (*She examines the flask*) We've given her more than half a flask full. That's enough to de-sensibilize an elephant. Something dreadful might happen to her.

Jimmy Well she deserves it.

Scattybags On the other hand, something nice might happen. She might become the exact opposite of what she is. I'd better find her, and I might need this.

Mrs Scattybags takes a white shawl from the trolley and hurries out. We hear the sound of a baby crying and Mrs Scattybags returns, delighted. She is carrying a baby

I was right, I was right! From being the most hateful thing in the world she's become the most lovable thing in the world. A baby! She's reverted right back to the time before she became evil. (*She pauses for thought*) It's a tragedy!

Jimmy A tragedy? How can a baby be a tragedy?

Scattybags You haven't seen what an ugly one she is. I do declare, she's the ugliest baby sister in the whole world. Here, take a look.

Mrs Scattybags tosses the baby to Jimmy, who catches it

Jimmy Careful!

Dad (*examining the baby*) Lots of little babies look rubbery.

Jimmy (*giving the baby back*) You've got to be very careful with babies, Mrs Scattybags.

Scattybags (*putting the baby in the trolley*) You're absolutely right. I knew this trolley would come in useful. I was a little bit sensible to keep it, wasn't I, Jimmy?

Jimmy Of course. And I'm sure you'll look after the baby better than anyone.

Dad (*finding the flask*) I think I'll have a gargle myself. I've been far too sensible all my life. (*He makes a business of gargling*)

More lights glitter

Wow! Look at all those people!

Dad waves to the audience, delighted to see them

Scattybags Well, I'd better be off then. And don't forget to make more of that antidote. I'm going to be far too busy from now on.

Jimmy I won't forget.

Jimmy walks her to the exit. Dad is sitting on the floor trying on a football boot and a flipper. He is feeling marvellous

Goodbye, Mrs Scattybags, goodbye.

Scattybags Oh I nearly forgot to say goodbye to the children. Goodbye, children!

Mrs Scattybags exits

Jimmy (*waving*) Look, there's Mum coming. (*Shouting*) Don't forget to show her the baby, Mrs Scatty.

Scattybags (*off*) I won't forget. Goodbye.

Dad is getting up from the floor

Jimmy Mum's coming, Dad. Dad, what on earth are you up to?

Dad I've still enough fizz in my old bones to swim the Channel single-handed and play football and do all the things I dreamed of doing before I took Dr Sensible's medicine. I've so much fizz in me I feel I could do them all at once.

Jimmy tosses a ball to Dad, which he neatly heads back

Jimmy And what about day-dreams, Dad. How do you feel about them now?

Dad Day-dreams and poetry, Jimmy. I wouldn't be without them. My, do I feel good. I think I'll have another little gargle.

Mum enters

Mum (*flustered*) Thank goodness you're safe. I've been worried sick about you. I've just seen Mrs Scattybags with her baby sister. (*Puzzled*) How can she be so old and have such a baby, baby sister?

Jimmy I'll explain later, Mum.

Dad Here, Mum, try this. (*He gives her the flask*) There's a teeny weeny bit left and it works wonders. Can I go out and play now?

Mum Of course you can.

Dad exits

(*To Jimmy*) What's up with your dad?

Jimmy Try that stuff and see.

Mum (*sniffing it*) I'll give it a try. (*She gargles*) Whoops! What a wonderful effect.

The lights glitter

I feel younger by yonks.

Dad rushes back in

Dad Did it work?

The telephone rings

Mum I can even hear bells ringing.

Dad It's the phone, Mum.

Mum picks up the phone and listens

Mum (*to Jimmy and Dad*) It's the Prime Minister.

Jimmy and Dad gather round the phone; concerned

(*On the phone*) What? . . . You've seen Dr Sensible in her pram? . . . And you've heard about everything our Jimmy's been up to?

Jimmy Tell the Prime Minister we're still going to make some more of the antidote.

Dad Yes, barrels and barrels of it.

Mum (*ignoring them*) What? . . . (*Astonished*) No!

Jimmy }
Dad } (*together*) No?

Mum (*with her hand over the mouthpiece*) The Prime Minister thinks Dr Sensible looked ridiculous in her pram. Everything's being unbanned. Birthdays. Christmas, telly, everything! And it's all because of our Jimmy.

Dad }
Jimmy } (*together*) Hurrah!

Mum (*with her hand over the mouthpiece*) Eh? . . . What? . . . Ooooooh, no!

Dad ⎱
Jimmy ⎰ (*together*) No??

Mum (*hand over the mouthpiece*) Yes!

Dad ⎱
Jimmy ⎰ (*together*) Yes? Hurrah!

Mum What marvellous news. (*She puts down the phone*) Tomorrow is going
to be National Gargling With Jelly Day. And the Prime Minister is going
to set an example by gargling with two pints of watery green jelly in front
of the entire Parliament. He's ashamed he ever listened to Dr Sensible.

Jimmy I don't believe it.

Mum It's true. And every child in the country will be given their favourite
flavoured jelly to gargle with.

Dad and Jimmy are playing football

Jimmy Great. Everything will be back to normal.

Mum Better than normal Jimmy. All Dr Sensible's medicine is being poured
away, and you're going to be made the Junior Minister for Fun! And
guess who's going to be made the Senior Minister for Fun?

Jimmy Mrs Scattybags?

Mum Yes. And this clinic, why it'll become a museum of horrors, a warning
against being too sensible too often. My, it's going to be a jelly nice world
to be in!

As many lights as possible are glittering

They all say their goodbyes and exit

CURTAIN

FURNITURE AND PROPERTY LIST

ACT I

SCENE 1

On stage: Nil

SCENE 2

On stage: Grey furniture
Grey pictures
Television
Telephone
Bed

Off stage: Toothbrush **(Jimmy)**
Book **(Jimmy)**

Personal: **Jimmy:** watch (worn throughout)

SCENE 3

On stage: Table. *On it:* breakfast bowls, cornflakes, morning paper
Cupboard, with petrol can in it
Balloon

Off stage: Handlebars **(Dad)**
Pitchfork **(Dr Sensible)**
Doctor's bag containing flask, phial, bottles etc. **(Dr Sensible)**
Sugar **(Jimmy)**
Trolley containing various pieces of junk **(Mrs Scattybags)**

Personal: **Dr Sensible:** matches, nurse's watch (worn throughout)

SCENE 4

On stage: Table. *On it:* breakfast bowls, cornflakes, morning paper

Off stage: Apple **(Jimmy)**
Magnifying glass **(Jimmy)**
Sack containing rubber gloves, bricks, hamburger, medicine, outsized
hypodermic needle **(Dr Sensible)**

SCENE 5

On stage: Bed
Telephone

Off stage: Torch **(Dr Sensible)**
Doctor's bag containing brushes, make-up pots etc. **(Dr Sensible)**
Stretcher **(Stage management)**

ACT II

SCENE 1

On stage: Bed
Bedpan
Soundproof screen
Mop
Cupboard containing walking sticks, surgical instruments, pillows, artificial limbs, laughing gas cylinder, surgical masks

Off stage: Body-sized trolley. *On it:* white sheet with zip, pieces of raw liver **(Dr Sensible)**
Small trolley. *On it:* large platter of surgical instruments **(Assistant)**
Plate of food **(Jimmy)**
Huge cake with practical flashing lights. *On it:* note **(Assistant)**

SCENE 2

As Scene 1

SCENE 3

On stage: Bits of junk
Litter
Dustbins
Bundle of clothes **(Stage management)**
Various notices

Off stage: Hypodermic needle **(Dr Sensible)**
Shopping bag containing 2 custard pies and a large dummy **(Mum)**
Foodstall. *On it:* fairylights, images of food, hamburger, folding table and chairs, cloth, candles, doughnuts, sweets **(Antonio)**

Personal: **Jimmy:** handkerchief
Jimmy: pair of shades
Policeman: handcuffs
Policeman: gum

SCENE 4

On stage: Phone
Jug of water
Football

Off stage: Doll **(Mrs Scattybags)**

Personal: **Jimmy:** catapult or water pistol
Mrs Scattybags: handkerchief

LIGHTING PLOT

Practical fittings required: bedside lamp

Various simple interior and exterior settings

ACT I, SCENE 1

To open: Spotlights as described

       No cues

ACT I, SCENE 2

To open: General interior lighting. TV flicker

Cue 1	**Mum** and **Dad** exit *Crossfade to bedroom area*	(Page 3)
Cue 2	**Jimmy** turns on a bedside light *Snap on practical with covering spot*	(Page 4)
Cue 3	**Jimmy** reads then dozes off *Change lighting*	(Page 4)
Cue 4	**Bodies:** ". . . it wants its own body back." (6th time) *Fade to Black-out*	(Page 5)

ACT I, SCENE 3

To open: General interior lighting

Cue 5	**Dr Sensible** lights a match and throws it out *Flame effect*	(Page 7)
Cue 6	**Jimmy** sits up and watches *Change lighting to lurid green*	(Page 7)
Cue 7	**Dr Sensible** returns the things to her bag *Change lights back to reality*	(Page 8)
Cue 8	**Dr Sensible:** ". . . loony nitbits letting her escape." *Spotlight on Prime Minister*	(Page 12)
Cue 9	**Prime Minister:** ". . . it it doesn't work on Jimmy Smith." *Black-out. Bring up spots as described*	(Page 12)
Cue 10	**Jimmy** exits *Fade to Black-out*	(Page 13)

ACT I, SCENE 4

To open: General interior lighting

| *Cue* 11 | **Jimmy:** "I bet the Queen hasn't." | (Page 16) |
| | *Slow lighting change* | |

| *Cue* 12 | **Jimmy:** "Or the King at least." | (Page 17) |
| | *Black-out. When ready, bring up spots* | |

| *Cue* 13 | **Jimmy:** ". . . nothing could wake me up." | (Page 17) |
| | *Fade to Black-out* | |

ACT I, SCENE 5

To open: Dim lighting

| *Cue* 14 | **Dr Sensible:** ". . . important part of my plan." | (Page 18) |
| | *Spot on Prime Minister* | |

| *Cue* 15 | **Prime Minister:** "An ambulance is on the way." | (Page 19) |
| | *Fade spot on Dr Sensible* | |

| *Cue* 16 | **Prime Minister:** ". . . the dreaded Morbillious Measels." | (Page 19) |
| | *Fade spot on Prime Minister and bring up strobe lighting and flashing blue lights. Fade when ready* | |

| *Cue* 17 | **Mrs Scattybags** looks around | (Page 19) |
| | *Fade to Black-out* | |

ACT II, SCENE 1

To open: Flashing lights

| *Cue* 18 | **Reporters** enter | (Page 20) |
| | *Fade flashing lights. Spots as described* | |

| *Cue* 19 | **Reporters** exit | (Page 20) |
| | *Lights up full* | |

| *Cue* 20 | **Dad:** ". . . we have to obey the rules." | (Page 23) |
| | *Change lighting* | |

| *Cue* 21 | **Jimmy** sits dejected on his bed | (Page 24) |
| | *Fade to Black-out* | |

ACT II, SCENE 2

To open: Dim lighting

| *Cue* 22 | **Assistant** switches on light | (Page 25) |
| | *Snap on light and covering spots* | |

| *Cue* 23 | **Dr Sensible:** ". . . that undisciplined and traitorous child." | (Page 27) |
| | *Black-out. When ready, spot on Reporter* | |

| *Cue* 24 | **Reporter** exits | (Page 27) |
| | *Black-out* | |

ACT II, Scene 3

To open: Grey lighting

Cue 25	**Dr Sensible:** "Get a move on!" *Flashing lights*	(Page 28)
Cue 26	**Mrs Scattybags:** "Come on, Jimmy, and stay close." *Fade lights. When ready, change lighting*	(Page 29)
Cue 27	**Policeman:** ". . . halt, come back!" *Lights cross-fade*	(Page 32)
Cue 28	**Antonio:** ". . . Music! Lights!" *Change lighting*	(Page 34)
Cue 29	**Dr Sensible** closes up the stall *Cross-fade to grey lighting*	(Page 35)

ACT II, Scene 4

To open "grey" lighting

Cue 30	**Dad** takes **Mrs Scattybags** to the edge of the stage *Follow spot on Mrs Scattybags*	(Page 38)
Cue 31	**Jimmy** gargles with jelly *Bring up bright lights*	(Page 39)
Cue 32	**Mrs Scattybags:** ". . . cruel and mean to children." *More lights sparkle*	(Page 39)
Cue 33	**Dad:** ". . . too sensible all my life." *More lights glitter*	(Page 40)
Cue 34	**Mum:** What a wonderful effect." *Lights glitter*	(Page 41)
Cue 35	**Mum:** ". . . a jelly nice world to be in!" *More lights glitter*	(Page 42)

EFFECTS PLOT

ACT I

ACT II

To open: Sirens. When ready, fade

Cue 18	**Jimmy** strains to see what is happening ... *Background sound of heartbeat*	(Page 20)
Cue 19	**Dr Sensible** pulls out a roundish red object *Heartbeat stops*	(Page 21)
Cue 20	**Dad:** "... we have to obey the rules." *Music*	(Page 23)
Cue 21	The top of the cake rises *Brief burst of fun-fair music*	(Page 25)
Cue 22	**Reporter** exits *Scene change music*	(Page 27)
Cue 23	**Jimmy:** "I promise and ..." *Dr Sensible music*	(Page 28)
Cue 24	**Dr Sensible:** "Get a move on!" *Sound of sirens*	(Page 28)
Cue 25	**Mrs Scattybags:** "Come on, Jimmy, and stay close." *Music*	(Page 29)
Cue 26	**Mum** and **Dad:** "Let's do it then." *Music*	(Page 31)
Cue 27	**Policeman:** "Oi! You can't do that!" *Cut music*	(Page 31)
Cue 28	**Mrs Scattybags:** "... Dr Sensible hasn't contaminated." *Sound of hand bell ringing off*	(Page 32)
Cue 29	**Jimmy:** "And—look!" *Fairground music*	(Page 32)
Cue 30	**Antonio:** "Music! Lights!" *Music*	(Page 34)
Cue 31	**Mrs Scattybags:** "... overpowers you completely." *Scene change music*	(Page 37)
Cue 32	**Jimmy:** "... amused by such rubbish." *Dr Sensible music*	(Page 37)
Cue 33	**Mrs Scattybags** hurries out *Sound of baby crying*	(Page 39)
Cue 34	**Dad:** "Did it work?" *Telephone*	(Page 41)

MADE AND PRINTED IN GREAT BRITAIN BY
LATIMER TREND & COMPANY LTD PLYMOUTH